PAST

BRISTOL

TIMES

22 fascinating episodes from
Bristol's rich history

Geoffrey Body

with additional material by
Roy Gallop and Ken Griffiths

FIDUCIA PRESS

2008

PAST BRISTOL TIMES

CONTENTS

The popularity of our series of three volumes of Past Somerset Times has encouraged the author and publishers to produce this first edition of Past Bristol Times. It follows the same pattern of selecting and describing some of the highlights from the past of an area incredibly well endowed with characters, incidents and achievements. The series is produced and distributed by community publishers Fiducia Press, 10 Fairfield Road, Bristol BS3 1LG and printed in Bristol by Doveton Press Ltd. The material in this work has been researched and written by Geoffrey Body with contributions by Roy Gallop and Ken Griffiths who have also undertaken the layout and design work. The contents of Past Bristol Times are copyright and may not be reproduced without written permission. The map on this page and on the cover is reproduced by kind permission of the Bristol Central Library.

FIDUCIA PRESS
ISBN 978 0 946217 32 8

A Pioneer Dock

'In 1712 a company of adventurous Bristolians resolved upon constructing a dock for the accommodation of shipping at Sea Mills.'

The remains of original buildings at the former Roman port of Abonae, now Sea Mills

At Sea Mills the modest River Trym joins the River Avon at a point on its north bank some five miles from Avonmouth and the Severn Estuary and just before the larger river enters the Avon Gorge and the dock complex at Bristol. The Romans quickly saw this as a suitable spot on the route from Silchester to Caerleon to locate a harbour, fort and trading centre which they called Portus Abonae. Traces of buildings from the first and second centuries have been found but not of the wharf at which the corn and other supplies would have been loaded onto the vessels that ferried them across to Wales. It might well have been overlaid by the pioneer wet dock that was built at Sea Mills early in the 18th century.

At that time the site at the end of the River Trym was owned by Edward Southwell of Kingsweston, a man of some substance who served for some fifteen years as a Tory MP for Bristol and became Secretary of State for Ireland. He agreed a 999 year lease of the land and a mill there to Bristol merchant Joshua Franklin for a payment of £81 per annum. Franklin would have been well aware of the problem of large vessels having to transfer their cargo to lighters for the journey up the Avon to the city and of the costs incurred by smaller ones which had to wait for the right state of the tide and then pay for several small boats and their rowers to tow them up river.

Possibly aware of earlier such projects in London and Liverpool, around 1712 Franklin came up with the idea of building an enclosed dock on his mill site so that vessels could load and discharge there without regard to the tides and also cut out the tortuous route up river to the city. By a partnership agreement dated 20 March 1716 Franklin took four fellow merchants as partners into the venture, John Spaul, John King, Lionel Lyde and Noblet Ruddock, and completed his dock in 1717 at a cost of £9,600

Noblet Ruddock was Sheriff of Bristol in 1721 and also had a share in the vessel *Dispatch* which left the city on a slaving trip in 1725. However, his ventures failed to prosper and two years later he left for the West Indies, a ruined and bankrupt man. The Sea Mills dock also soaked up most of Franklin's fortune and in 1726 the original partnership was forced to take in Walter King, Samuel Jacob, and Peter(?) Day. They took some of the 32 shares in the Sea Mills Dock Company whose assets by this time included a crane and engines, warehouses and a storehouse.

Unhappily this pioneer dock venture was not a success. Moving goods on to Bristol by wagon or packhorse was slow and costly, while completing the journey by barge also meant transhipment and dependence on the tides to access the dock. In both cases the extra costs more than swallowed up the benefits of the improvement in ship turnround times. The Sea Mills Dock did, however, continue in use and its shipping was one of the targets which a gang of extortionists threatened to burn in 1730. One of the dock's later uses was as a fitting out point for privateers during the mid-18th century wars, but the enterprise was clearly not fulfilling its original high expectations.

In 1750 a change of fortune for the dock seemed to be a possibility when city merchants formed a joint stock company to establish a whaling business. The Whale Fishery Company fitted out two ships, the *Bristol* and the *Adventure,* and these landed five whales in1752, the boiling also taking placed there. The *St Andrew* was also engaged in the whaling activity but not all the sailings were as successful as the first ones and the company went out of business in 1761.

Sea Mills Dock was now in serious decline. Bankrupt potter Daniel Saunders of Westbury-on-Trym was desparately trying to sell three shares in the venture in 1772 and 'spacious warehouses' were still being offered for rent in1798 but it seems that very little dock activity took place after 1775. Today only some entrance masonry remains to mark this pioneer dock enterprise and only small private boats moor within the original walls.

The stout masonry of the entrance to Sea Mills Dock has survived for nearly 300 years.

The Railwaymen's Friend

Born 1841   Died 1927
Miss Emma Saunders

"The Railwaymen's Friend"

Erected by railway workers and friends in grateful remembrance of her fifty years devoted Christian service

(Text of a rather faded memorial tablet on the outer wall of the entrance to Temple Meads train station.)

When Emma Saunders reached her 80th birthday on 2 March 1921 over 5,000 local railwaymen clubbed together to mark the occasion with gifts of an illuminated address, a settee and an armchair. Such was the regard in which this lady was held for her forty years of kindness towards railwaymen in every grade, company and job in the Bristol area. The presentation to her was made by the local GWR Divisonal Superintendent who paid tribute to the untiring devotion of Miss Saunders and the team of like-minded ladies she led. No doubt he also suggested that she had earned the right to relax on the settee or in the armchair knowing full well that she was highly unlikely to do so.

In her youth Emma Saunders had worked with the girls of a Bristol industrial home and with the pupils of a Ragged School. Then, when Miss Louisa Stevenson had to give up helping rail staff and their families as a result of ill health, Miss Saunders took over the role and helped to set up the Railway Mission which began its work in 1881. Her original territory embracing the Clifton Extension Railway, the route to the Severn Tunnel and around Pyle Hill quickly expanded to cover not only all the lines and stations in the Bristol area but also the various sheds and works, the dockside cranes, cartage depots and the like. This remarkable lady and her helpers were even given passes which allowed them to travel on locomotives and in goods vans, a rare and remarkable recognition of their value to the railway community.

Emma Saunders and her Railway Mission set up the Bristol & West of England Railwaymen's Institute to provide an alternative to the temptations of licensed premises and strong drink. Instead it offered a canteen, facilities for billiards, bagatelle and skittles and a room for educational and religious meetings. But what really endeared Emma Saunders to the staff of the Great Western and Midland Railways was her very personal activities like visiting families in trouble, taking flowers to give away as button-holes or for brightening a workplace, the well-meaning tracts she handed out and the many kindly words and encouragement which were never stinted. To the men who collected and delivered railway goods traffic by horse and dray, for example, she gave a copy of *Black Beauty* and an admonition to treat their horses well.

'The Railwayman's Friend', as this remarkable lady was known, died in 1927. Four uniformed railwaymen carried her coffin through Clifton from Sion Hill to Christ Church followed by a vast crowd of railway staff of every grade and each one wearing a daffodil in his buttonhole in memory of the untiring kindness of an old friend. Not that the story ends there for the recreational facilities provided by the Rail Mission survived in the form of the British Railways Staff Association and the individual Railway Missioners continued to give practical and spiritual help into the era of the modern railway. The plaque erected to the memory of Emma Saunders can still be seen outside Temple Meads station.

Magistrates Memorandum 1520

Turkeys, carps, hops, piccards and beer
Came into England all in one year.

"Whereas it hath been complained that the brewers of this town have used heretofore to take home again to their houses from their customers being tapsters within the town all such ale as hath been turned fusty, dead and unable to be drunken within three days after the clearing of the same, which unwholesome ale the brewers of craft and sublety have tried to put among the ale at the next brewing, and do so to utter the same unto the king's people within this town, whereby it is likely that some persons heretofore hath taken infection and disease. It is therefore enacted the sixteenth of October, in the year above written, that it shall not be lawful to any such brewers to take any refused ale, but that the same so found faulty be forthwith cast into the street before the door of the same customer or tapster, by the oversight of the sergeant of the ward where such default is found."

"Each brewer in default of the above observance to be fined in a penalty of 20s., and the tapster 3s. 4d. – half to the sheriffs and the other half to the chamber. Also that any brewer using 'hops' in his ale except in the months of June, July, and August, to forfeit for every default 40s. to be disposed of as above."

A Well-Planned Abduction

'Schoolgirl and surgeon - elopement and chase to Gretna Green'

A court case heard before the Recorder Sir Vicary Gibbs on 14 April 1794 was destined to become the talk of Bristol. On that day Richard Vining Perry, a young surgeon of high standing and respectable family, was put on trial for abducting and marrying Clementina Clerke, a young lady of just fourteen years and eleven months.

Miss Clerke was an heiress whose uncle had amassed a fortune in Jamaica and left most of it to her when he died in 1791. He had also placed her in a very proper school kept by Miss Mills, a protege of the redoubtable Hannah More. The rich young pupil was described as very beautiful but somewhat precocious.

It seems that on two occasions when the young Clementina was out with her fellow pupils on the Downs her path had crossed that of Richard Perry who had offered her a courtly bow. He had also written her two notes, the second proposing elopement to which she had readily, if surprisingly, agreed. The notes had been smuggled into and out of the school with the help of a school servant, Betty Baker, and it was she who was to play a vital role in the lovers' plans.

On 18 March 1791, less than two months after her rich uncle had died, a furtive conversation between the lovesick schoolgirl and Betty Baker was followed by the latter leaving the school on an errand and failing to return. What did happen was that two days later a chaise arrived at the school gates with a liveried servant alighting and seeking out the schoolmistress with a letter purporting to be from Clementina's guardian. It read 'William Gordon's compliments to Miss Mills, requests she will send Miss Clerke in the Chaise to his house, as a relation of hers is just arrived and wishes to see her.' To maintain credibility the clever conspirators even invited Miss Mills to go with her pupil, no doubt knowing that such a course would be impracticable when the lady had a school to run.

Once in the waiting chaise, Miss Clerke was whisked off to Infirmary Street and Mr Perry's house. There she was joined by Betty Baker, probably prepared with clothes and other necessities for the adventure to come. At Stokes Croft turnpike the two ladies joined Mr Perry and a friend of his called Bayton, climbed into waiting a post-chaise and four and set off at speed for Gretna Green.

When Clementina Clerke failed to return to school and was proved not to have gone to Mr Gordon's home an anxious Miss Mills was able to piece together the facts of the melodrama. Joined by her brother and Mr Weeks of the Bush Tavern they set off in pursuit and in the middle of Cumberland met the newly-married Mr and Mrs Perry returning from Gretna Green. They tried to talk to the bride but Perry was having none of it and, as the report put it, 'at once took her on the continent.'

The interval between elopement and court case suggests that the Perry couple took their time before returning to Bristol but then found that they had not been forgotten. Richard Perry was arraigned but escaped the possibility of severe sentence when his wife said that 'she was perfectly satisfied and never for one moment wished to leave her husband.' A lot of shouting greeted the 'Not Guilty' verdict but Perry and his young wife went free to enjoy a less dramatic existence.

A News First

For over a century newspapers suffered from limitations of the printing process, poor communications and transport and government fears that the spread of news would encourage sedition From 1712 until 1855 rising stamp duty and taxes kept pushing up costs thus limiting newspapers to a weekly edition. Bristol had six of these, four of which came out on Saturday, but few daily newspapers existed anywhere outside London

It took the vision of Scottish businessman Peter Macliver and Newcastle journalist Walter Reid to give Bristol the West's first daily, the *Western Daily Press*. A modest affair, it first appeared on 1 June 1858 priced at one penny and with 27 agents around the city prepared to 'deliver copies to any address in Bristol, Clifton or the adjacent suburbs.'

In 1877 the *Bristol Evening News* was added to give the city its first evening newspaper. Eight years later the two newspapers moved from the original premises in Broad Street to a larger home in Baldwin Street shown above decorated for the coronation of King Edward VII.

Wife for Sale

Come all you kind husbands who have scolding wives'
Who thro' living together are tired of your lives,
If you cannot persuade her nor good natur'd make her
Place rope round her neck & to market pray take her.

Until the passing of the Matrimonial Clauses Act of 1857 ordinary people had no real chance of a lawful remedy for dissolving a marriage that had broken down. However for at least two centuries before that date there had been a quite widespread belief that a wife could legitimately be disposed of by offering her for sale, provided this was done by leading her with a halter round her neck to a public place, auctioning her there and having the transaction witnessed by a person of some standing. In some cases this would even be a churchwarden with the event formally recorded in the parish register. Around the country several hundred unrewarding marriages were ended in this manner with Thomas Hardy giving the practice classical status when, in the first few pages of *The Mayor of Casterbridge,* hay-trusser Michael Henchard sold his wife for five guineas

Two handbills printed in Bristol provide lurid details of two examples of wife-selling which took place in the 1820s. One of these revealed the fairly common feature of existing infidelity with the auction then being used to give the situation a form of legitimacy. Under the title *A Ready way to get ride of a BAD WIFE'* one pamphlet described the case thus:-

'On Thursday the 28th November 1822, a very novel transaction took place in our market; about half past eleven o'clock, by which time many live beasts had changed masters, into the market popp'd a jolly son of Crispin with his better half genteelly led by him in

a halter, for the purpose of disposing of her in the same manner as other gentlemen dispose of livestock when they have no farther occasion for them. It appeared that they had lived a most uncomfortable life for a length of time, the husband ruling her, (not with a rod of iron) but with a strap of leather, with which he used to alter the colour of her beautiful hide, till it displayed as many glowing colours as the rain bow. By her drunkenness and extravagance he was at length reduced to his Last, as he had absolutely spent his all, and he declared her upon his sole (soul) that he could no longer vamp up his credit, and therefore, he having a heart as hard as his lap-stone, he declared, that although they were united as close as sole and upper-leather yet that they were entirely out of welt; and that a separation must immediately take place; fully aware that he could not dispose of her by private contract, she agreed to be exposed to public sale in the market, with a halter about her neck; Crispin nothing loth, took her at her word, and brought her to market, where the first bidding was made by a horse-dealer, who offered half-a-crown; 5s. said a pig-jobber, 10s. says a publican, 15s. says a rough country wap straw; £1 said a butcher, who it is supposed had trespassed upon the premises before. No one seemed anxious to advance on this price, and they adjourned to a public-house, where the money was paid, the bargain delivered to the purchaser, who took her to an old clothes shop, not a hundred miles from the Temple church, where he rigged her afresh and took her home, leaving Crispin to the enjoyment of his pot and pipe.

Six months after this event another case of wife-selling proceeded much less smoothly. It began when drover John Nash of Rosemary Street led his wife in a halter to the Thomas Street Market on 29 May 1822, a curious and excited crowd following at his heels. At a spot opposite the Bell Yard he announced that he wished to auction his wife and was ready to receive bids for her. This stunned the crowd but eventually, largely out of pity, a young man tentatively offered sixpence. Despite Nash's assurances that his wife had many qualities and was 'sound, and free from vice' no more offers were forthcoming and the deal was duly done.

Mrs Nash seems to have liked the look of her buyer and appeared quite satisfied with the transaction but he was having second thoughts and offered her up again. With some relief he accepted a bid of ninepence, pocketed his profit and handed the lady over. However she, 'not taken with her purchaser', had other ideas and fled the scene with her mother. Seeing his bargain running away, the new buyer chased after them but, when captured, the two ladies insisted on putting the matter to a magistrate who quickly dismissed the case. While all this was going on the crowd had turned on the man behind the unsavoury affair and compelled John Nash to beat a hasty retreat, wifeless and just sixpence better off.

The verse in the heading is followed by others and finally concludes:-

> *Here's success to this couple to keep up the fun,*
> *May bumpers go round at the birth of a son,*
> *Long life to them both, and in peace & content,*
> *May their days and their nights for ever be spent.*

The Bewitchment of Molly and Dobby Giles

And 'a remedy which modern delicacy will not permit to be described.'

In 1747 a journey from London to Bristol by wagon cost around ten shillings and took six days. It was not something to be undertaken lightly for the unsprung wagon was highly uncomfortable and by the time the cost of luggage at a penny a pound had been added, plus a shilling a night for overnight stays at a hedge inn, there would be little left out of a sovereign except sore bones and bruising. Not that this would have overly concerned Richard Giles of the Lamb Inn at Lawford's Gate, for he was the Bristol agent for the service and happily collected his fee for booking passengers and goods.

Clearly an enterprising fellow, Giles later went into the carrier business for himself and ran a very successful service between Bristol and Bath. Around 1760 he became

Ordinary people could not afford stage coach travel and had little choice but to use the carrier's wagon which would be cheap but extremely uncomfortable.

determined to expand by offering a 'flying wagon' service to London which would cut the journey time down to just three days. This was not a popular move with existing carriers on the route but soon Richard Giles had something more serious to worry about when his 13-year old daughter Molly and her younger sister, 8-year old Dobby, suddenly showed all the signs of being bewitched. By the end of 1871 a serious of bizarre events which began to afflict the unhappy girls had become a *cause celebre* in Bristol.

Among those who investigated the extraordinary goings-on at the Lamb Inn was Mr Henry Durbin, a prosperous and well-respected druggist of Recliff Street. He later described how the youngsters had been bitten and scratched while lying in their beds and were later thrown from them. The girls were pricked with pins, Molly's cap ripped off and something started drumming on their bed. Foul voices and threats were also to be heard and furniture was hurled about the room. A Major Drax was present on one occasion when the terrified youngsters were raised towards the ceiling. Along with his coachman and footman and Mr Durbin himself, the burly soldier attempted to stop this happening but they found that 'four stout men could scarce hold one child'.

Before long a number of other eminent gentlemen had joined Durbin in trying to understand and remedy the situation. He had already got the evil spirit to respond to questions by knocks and scratches and, to everyone's astonishment, it answered equally well when the visiting clergymen tried it with Latin, Greek and Hebrew. The Rev.J.Camplin, precentor of the Cathedral, even tried posing questions mentally and also got the right answers.

While all this was going on Richard Giles was faring no better than his daughters. Mr Durbin had already got the spirit to admit that it had been sent by an old witch living at Mangotsfield. She, apparently, had been paid by a rival carrier to bewitch not only the Giles family but his business as well, and was making a thorough job of it. A Giles wagon and its seven horse team got totally stuck for sixteen hours at Hanham and was only shifted by using a further eighteen horses. At the same spot the chains of other teams broke without apparent cause and were mysteriously twisted into knots. Finally, when the carrier himself was driving home from Bath in his gig, his harness broke at exactly the same place as the earlier events and a malevolent old lady appeared briefly beside the wheel of the vehicle. Profoundly disturbed by all that had happened Richard Giles died four days later.

Poor Richard Giles and his 'advisors' had tried everything to resolve the bewitchment. The Rev. Symes had offered prayers in St Werburgh's Church and seen some of his parishioners walk out in protest. Molly was sent away to Swansea for a while and things improved but were then even worse when she got back. The spirit apparently admitted that it had received a further ten guineas to continue the offensive. Patrons were deserting the Lamb Inn because of its frightening reputation and after the death of its landlord his widow decided that the time had come for drastic action. In disguise, so as not to give too much away, a deputation called upon another old lady, known as the 'Cunning Woman of Bedminster', and asked for her help. Without any prompting she professed full knowledge of the situation and, to quote the chronicler, 'propounded a remedy of his (the spirit's) overthrow which modern delicacy will not permit to be described.' No matter, it worked.

We are variously told that Giles suspected his workmen to have had a hand in the wagon incidents and that his wife and mother-in-law were part of the plot in order to buy the inn cheaply. Some aspects of this saga bear a remarkable resemblance to more recent cases of poltergeist activity but past accounts of events such as these are notably prone to embellishment and exaggeration and the truth will never be known.

16th Century Glimpses

'Paid the wrestlers on both sides, 4s. The old custom was 6s. 8d., but for because the country side brought not a goose according to the old custom, therefore was paid but 4s.
!!!!!!!!!!!!!!

'After dinner, the said Mayor, Sheriff, and their brethren to assemble at the Mayor's compter, there waiting the bishop's coming, playing the meanwhiles at dice. The town clerk to find them dice, and to have one
!!!!!!!!!!!!!!

penny of every raffle.
!!!!!!!!!!!!!!!!!!!!

'Paid to Savage, the foot post, to go to Wellington with a letter to the Recorder touching the holding of Sessions, and if not there to go to Wimborne Minster, where he has a house, where he found him, and returned with a letter; which post was six days upon that journey in very foul weather, and I paid him for his pains 13s. 4d.'
!!!!!!!!!!!!!!!

Explosion at Bathurst Basin

All in a policeman's day

When PC 117A Webber booked on duty on 21 November 1888 it seemed just like any other day on early shift. He was attached to the river police and his beat included Bristol's Floating Harbour, always a busy place full of shipping and the movement of people and cargoes. Today his route included Bathurst Basin where the Jersey ketch *United* was anchored along with a couple of other sailing vessels and the steam tug *Sprite.*

The *United* had been loaded at Welsh Back with some 300 barrels of naptha carted in from Brislington, and then towed to Bathurst Basin by the *Sprite.* Because of the volatile nature of her cargo the ketch had been kept in the entrance lock overnight but was now just inside the basin and hoping to sail as soon as the strong winds eased

Webber paid a routine visit to the *United* and chatted with her crew, Henry Cartwright the master, Joseph Cartwright the mate, crew member Joseph Basle and the lad Toby. He noted the 50tons of naptha stored aft and understood why the volatile nature of the cargo was making everyone nervous. The master had banned any sort of flame. There was to be no smoking, cooking or even tea-making.

Skipper Henry Cartwright was clearly anxious to get the *United* to sea and to get his dangerous cargo delivered in London and out of his ship. Sensitive to the pervading atmosphere Webber wished him well and resumed his rounds. Later he would have difficulty in believing that the normal peaceful scene he had seen could change so suddenly and so violently and that three of the seamen he had been talking to would be dead.

Just after 11am, as the policeman later recorded the time in his report, the whole area was rocked by an incredible explosion. In the basin itself ships' timbers and pieces of rigging were hurled high into the air accompanied by what a witness described as 'a high wall of flame of appalling fierceness' followed by 'a cloud of smoke of the blackest description.' At the centre of the inferno was the hapless *United* from which burning barrels of naptha spread outwards over the surface of the dock and congealed into a raft of flame which was driven towards the other vessels by the wind. These, too, were soon on fire from end to end with the flames rising to masthead height and higher.

Around the basin the hospital lost all its lower windows in the blast with the Ostrich pub and the houses in Guinea Street suffering the same fate. The huge blast wave also affected Robinson's Oil & Cake Mills on the opposite side of Bathurst Basin. The clerks there suffered the indignity of being blown off their stools but one of them recovered quickly enough to speed off to the premises of the river police who then telephoned Bridewell for assistance. A squad of policemen soon arrived to help the rescuers and the volunteer firemen from Fry's packing case factory and to control the increasing number of spectators.

The city fire brigade too was quickly on the scene with the engine making a dramatic arrival drawn by what the newsmen labelled 'splendid Grays'. The docks water float steamed into position near the outer harbour lock and together the appliances pumped water onto the burning vessels and scorched buildings which gave off great clouds of steam as a result. More hoses had

Bathurt Basin viewed from the lock entrance to the Avon New Cut.

to be brought in before the flames in the basin and on its stricken vessels could be brought under control after nearly three terrible hours.

Amidst all the carnage human dramas were also being played out. The *United's* able seaman who had been blown 40 yards into the water was spotted by a boat from the *Mary* manned by Captain James Everet and Mr James Moore a lay missionary. When two labourers in another small boat turned up to help they left Joseph Basle to them and tried to break into the forecastle of the burning *United* where its remaining crew were trapped. But the heat was too great and, badly singed, they were forced to leave the sailors to their sad fate

PC Webber had little time in which to take in the scene which he had earlier found so peaceful and which was now a wild, burning place of carnage and devastation. When the explosion occurred he had been struck in the chest by a piece of burning timber but, despite being in considerable pain, had tried to rescue the crew he had been chatting to just a short time earlier. Other heroes were Thomas Bevan and Sidney Gillard who had plunged into the dock to aid an 8-year Bedminster boy who had been accidentally pushed into the water. The youngster was clinging to the dock wall but seemed likely to lose his precarious hold until Bevan arrived to support him..

In addition to the damage to the buildings around the dock the intense heat had twisted one of the footbridges into an unrecognisable shape. However, before the day was out the damage to the hospital was being attended to by 'a battalion of glaziers' summoned from all over the city and intent on restoring the building to good order. The injured survivor was treated there for broken limbs and a head wound caused by a flaming spar

By 2 o'clock the fires were finally out but the scars of the tragedy would long remain.

On 4 July 1776 the American Congress passed its Declaration of Independence. The war that followed was clearly going to have a major effect on British ports but little did Bristol expect that in the following year one facet of the conflict was going to strike right at its heart. One man, in the pay of the Americans, brought the war into the very centre of the city as part of his plan to spy on and cripple British ships, ports and dockyards. With our home ports crowded with timber sailing vessels and lined with bulging warehouses they were especially vulnerable to an arsonist.
And such was......

Jack the Painter

Bristol City Docks c1900

For a short period at the beginning of 1777 Bristol was brought to a state of great alarm and near panic by the activities of a determined and ruthless arsonist. At times only hours separated the outbreak of one fire from the attempt to start another and very soon the whole inner city was in a high state of alert with the militia called in and bands of citizens organised to patrol vulnerable areas. With so many timber vessels, warehouses and dwellings packed closely together the fire risks in the city were always high, flames spread easily and often outran the firefighting capacity.

The trouble began during the night of 16 January. The tide was at its lowest and a host of vessels sat on the mud of the harbour, the work of loading and unloading halted until daybreak. Careful not to disturb the watchmen and any crew members who had not gone ashore, a dark figure had climbed aboard the *Savannah la Mar*, already loaded with goods for Jamaica, and set about his sinister task. Some of the tar and pitch which every sailing vessel carried had been spread around the mizzen mast and set alight. It took hold quickly and spread to the rigging before the alarm was raised and the blaze contained thanks to two water containers fortunately available on deck. The arsonist had already moved on to repeat his work on the Irish vessel *Hibernia* and the privateer *Fame* but in both cases the fires there failed to take hold.

Only a few hours later another arson attempt was discovered. This time the intruder had scaled a 10ft wall around the Corn Street warehouse of druggist James Morgan, levered out three iron window bars and then filled a box with a mixture of tar, turpentine and other combustibles. This was placed near some barrels of oil and an incendiary device set alight and left to do its work. Again the fire failed to take hold but the attempt sent a stark warning signal to the merchants of Bristol.

Three days passed without further incident and then, in the quiet early hours of a Sunday morning, the warning became a dreadful reality. Flames were spotted in Bell Lane where the grain and wool warehouse of Lawsley, Partridge & Company was soon well alight. Fire engines rushed to the scene and pumped river water onto the conflagration but neither the warehouse nor its neighbouring buildings could be saved. Such of the warehouse contents as were rescued were taken to the Exchange and Queen Square and placed under military guard.

In nearby Broad Street several fires were discovered at the Bell Inn and the whole of the Small Street and Corn Street areas were, for a while, under threat. As if this was not enough, two more arson attempts were found in a sugar house in Lewin's Mead and long torches, clearly intended for fire raising, at several other places.

By now the whole of Bristol was aware that it had a determined and indiscriminate fireraiser in its midst. Street patrols were hurriedly organised and a reward offered for the capture of the mysterious wrongdoer, the King adding £1,000 to this from his privy purse. The culprit's identity and motives formed a major topic of conversation with various interests blaming one another and others suspecting American involvement for hostilities with the colonists had begun less than a year earlier and there were still mixed opinions about the conflict. Although the Society of Merchant Venturers took a leading part in the hunt for the arsonist his activities did, ironically, help to quell the antagonism towards the regulations which required inflammable cargoes to be dealt with at the Society's newly improved and extremely expensive Merchants' Dock.

After several crisis weeks suspicions became focused on a Scot who had taken a succession of rooms in the Pithay but subsequently disappeared. He was eventually identified after a burglary in Lancashire and taken to London for questioning. The man was James Aitken, alias Jack the Painter, and after initially refusing to admit guilt later confessed to a visitor that he was the person who had set fire to the rope house in Portsmouth.

At Aitken's trial at Winchester on 6 March 1777 part of the evidence against him was his trademark incendiary device. One had been found at Portmsouth and consisted of a box of combustible material which was ignited by a candle after a measured period of burning. It was revealed that Aitken had also tried to start dockyard fires at Chatham and Plymouth and that he had gathered a great deal of data on naval vessels and establishments around the country. His aim was to deal a blow to Britain's maritime strength, all at the instigation of a member of the American Congress visiting Paris.

Condemned to death, Aitken was taken aboard the frigate *Arethusa* at Portsmouth and hanged from its mizzen mast, 67ft above a deck typical of those he had tried to set on fire in Bristol.

The British Coffee House

Here wise Remarkers on the Church and State
O'er Turkish Lap and smoaky Whiffs debate.
Here half shut Authors in Confusion lye,
And kindling Stuffs for Party Heats supply.

In these words one writer captured something of the nature of coffee houses in Bristol in the 18th century. They were the meeting places for writers, merchants and politicians, centres for the dissemination of news and gossip and always alive with conversation, the strong aroma of coffee and the pungent haze of cigar smoke. From early morning onwards the regulars would arrive, order the first dish of coffee of the day and settle down to greet and discourse with their friends and acquaintances. They would study the notices of sailings, auctions and other events on the walls and read the latest political and trade news once the newspapers arrived. For the penny cost of a cup of Mocha any reputable person could join this convivial society and gain much from the association.

The British Coffee House was a prime example of its kind and its position in Broad Street next to the equally notable White Lion Hotel made it popular and busy. From the White Lion and the nearby White Hart the *Monarch* and *Regulator* stage coaches carried passengers and luggage to and from London. Together the group kept Broad Street humming with the activity of carriages, chaises, horses and ostlers and with passengers, pedestrians, footmen and porters.

Coffee started arriving from India around 1610 and, after a slow start, the coffee house habit grew rapidly in London around the middle of the 17th century. By 1665 coffee was being sold in Bristol with the city's first coffee house then opening around 1677. This was the Elephant in All Saints Lane. Others followed and were soon rivalling taverns as centres for the discussion of business. Shipbuilders talked to ship owners there, manufacturers talked to merchants and even professional men like lawyers and financiers found the arrangement more congenial that using an office. So popular did coffee houses become that authority became worried that the disaffected might be plotting there and radicals spreading their uncomfortable brands of free thinking. There were even suggestions that the mayor ought to approve any reading matter appearing in the city's coffee houses.

The war between Britain and her American colonies was the subject of divided opinions here and the White Lion was noted as a gathering point for those Bristolians who supported the conflict. Their views were so strongly held that at one point effigies of two prominent Americans were tarred and feathered and then hung outside the tavern. At this point the neighbouring coffee house was known as the American Coffee House but as life returned to normal after the Treaty of Paris it saw advantage in changing its name to the British Coffee House.

The coffee house thrived during a major part of the 18th century, lasting from the rapid expansion of the 1720s onwards until

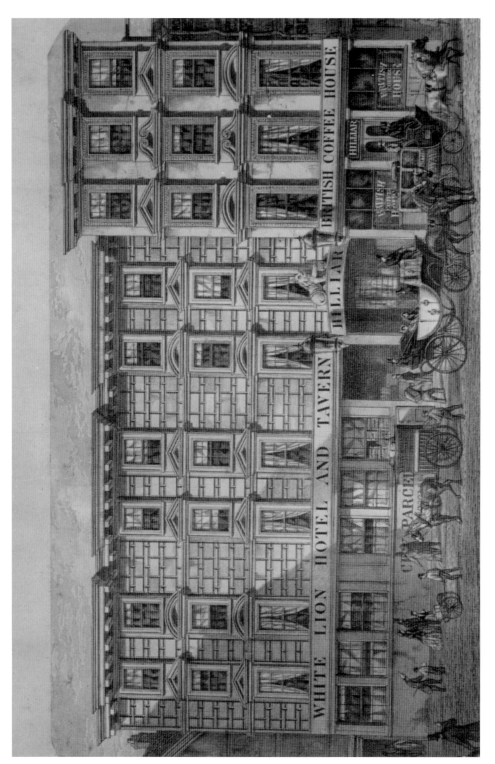

Broad Street Bristol

a decline began around 1780. The names they used very often denoted the prime interests of those that used them, names such as the West Indian Coffee House near the Exchange, the African in Prince's Street, the Marine in Queen Square and the Hot Well Coffee House for those taking the waters. Their decline was partly due to many hotels introducing their own coffee rooms forcing the coffee houses to move towards other activities such becoming salerooms. Fashion was also turning to tea as the drink of the times and by 1798 only four coffee houses survived in the city.

The Knee Brothers

In 1839 this pioneer removal firm set up their business at 26 Temple Street, Bristol. In the same year the infant Great Western Railway had reached Twyford and was to be opened through to Bristol two years later. The Knee Brothers saw this as an opportunity and came up with the idea of a container that could be loaded with furniture, horse-drawn to the station and then conveyed on a rail wagon to its final destination. Knee's Furniture Van 'For the removal of furniture etc without packing' was the forerunner of a long connection with railways and of the railway's own size-able container activity

Knee Brothers later took over premises in Boyce's Avenue, Clifton which had started life as the 'Royal Bazaar and Winter Gardens' built in a grand and ornate style by amateur architect Joseph King. But the-money ran out, the shops in the mall never opened and King's dream was never to be realised.

King's Arcade remained empty and desolate for a long time after closure in the 1980s but was then very pleasantly restored to the splendour pictured here a few year ago.

The Unlucky Visitor

'A man named Power, son of a Dublin attorney, happened to be in Bristol. Being a stranger and in poor circumstances, he fell under suspicion......'

This man Power was unlucky enough to be in Bristol at the end of 1730 when a series of serious extortion attempts created a period of high tension in the city. On the flimsiest of evidence he was to suffer greatly as a consequence and spend a long and cruel period in prison solely because of an extremely doubtful accusation and the fact that he was in poor circumstances and looked somewhat suspicious as a consequence.

The matter all started with a nasty and audacious outbreak of multiple extortion which had probably been going on for some time before it became public knowledge. It took the form of a spate of threatening letters thrown into shops or warehouses in the docks and central city areas. These notes stated that the premises would be burned down and the owner killed unless the writers were bought off with money. Secrecy was enjoined and instructions given for delivery of the extortion payment. There is little doubt that villains were being quietly paid off for some time before their efforts finally came to light and put the city in uproar.

The catalyst for the wave of panic that now engulfed Bristol was a serious fire in October 1730 which burned down the house of a Mr George Packer. Both he and his neighbour had received threats and chosen to ignore them.

The extortioners' next letter mentioned the Packer incident and vowed he would not escape them. Another threatened to set the whole city on fire. Packer himself fled to a house in Canons' Marsh, next to a warehouse containing hemp and cordage, and must have been severely shaken when that building too was subjected to an arson attempt. Bristolians were by now seriously alarmed. The watch was doubled, volunteers rushed forward to operate patrols, and a reward of £500 was offered for the detection of the people behind these atrocities. The extortion practice must have worked well in some cases for there were soon imitators in other cities. Soldiers had to be used to try to protect potentially vulnerable locations. There were also the usual attempts by one political party to blame those of a different persuasion.

Situations of the sort experienced in Bristol in 1730 tended to lead to high anxiety and panic and a frantic search for scapegoats, whether guilty or not. Several people were arrested and lodged in the gaols in Bristol, Bath and Ilchester, often on the flimsiest of suspicions. Poor Mr Power was one of these. A young girl thought she had seen him throw a letter into a shop and two others maintained that he had given them letters to throw into Mr Packer's house. This was enough to have the unfortunate fellow committed and not only taken to Newgate but there placed in the Pit, a dark and sinister underground chamber where condemned convicts were normally kept.

When at last he came to trial almost twelve months after his arrest, Power revealed that he spent over three months in chains without light, heat or visitors. After two ladies provided him with an alibi he was finally released through lack of convincing evidence but had to pay the gaoler's fees before walking free.

It seems unlikely that the unfortunate Irishman ever visited Bristol again!

First Across the Gorge

*Work on the Clifton Suspension Bridge
was started in 1831 but it was not
until 1864 that the century-old dream
of spanning the dramatic Avon Gorge was
finally realised.*

The Clifton Suspension Bridge has been a distinctive feature of the Bristol scene since its opening in 1864 but the early history of the structure was quite chequered. The idea of linking Clifton and Leigh Woods without descending the Avon Gorge to the river level below found its first concrete expression in the 1753 will of Bristol wine merchant William Vick. He 'had heard that the building of a bridge was practicable and might be completed for less than £10,000' and arranged for a sum of £1,000 to be paid to the Society of Merchant Venturers and invested by them for that purpose.

Nothing then happened until the building boom in Clifton in the 1790s when one William Bridge published a highly-fanciful bridge design in which a huge central arch was flanked by six stories of rooms and galleries and topped by a 700ft roadway. The rooms were to cater for everything from a market to a marine school and the structure had its own windmills and lighthouse!

The first realistic moves to implement the idea of a bridge across the gorge were made in 1829 with work on the project starting in 1831 only to be halted by the Bristol Riots. Various difficulties, especially of funding, then dogged a period of over twenty years until Brunel's death in 1859 prompted a new initiative to complete the work which he had once called 'my first child, my darling'.

There seems to have been a crossing of the Avon Gorge of a sort in 1825 when an American named Courtney 'flew' across

BRIDGE UNDER CONSTRUCTION.
A. SHOWING STAGING ON WHICH CHAINS WERE LAID. AUGUST 1863.
B&C. THE ROADWAY UNDER CONSTRUCTION 1864 SHOWING GIRDERS, AND SADDLES ON TOP OF PIERS.
D. THE OPENING CEREMONY DEC. 8TH. 1864.
I.K.BRUNEL, ENGINEER.

CLIFTON SUSPENSION BRIDGE

"The climb to the top of the Clifton tower of the suspension bridge was extremely nerve-racking but this view made it well worthwhile." (Author)

using a rope stretched from the windmill on the Clifton side to the heights on the opposite side of the river.

Of more substance was the linking of the two sides of the gorge when work on Brunel's bridge was restarted in 1836. This was done by making up an 800ft long bar by joining sections of 1.5in diameter iron lengths on the Leigh side and then using a capstan to drag this across to Clifton. Unfortunately one of the haulage cables broke in the transfer process, the bar fell into the river and got bent and the laborious business of getting it across the gorge had to be restarted.

The installation of the iron bar was the beginning of the main process of linking the two bridge piers. It was fitted with a roller from which a carrying basket was suspend-ed and this was used to move construction materials to wherever they were required. The bar being lower in the centre, the basket could descend under its own weight for the first part of its crossing and then be hauled up the slope on the rising section. An unauthorised crossing nearly ended in disaster when the basket stuck at the bend and a trailing rope became entangled with the masthead of the steamer *Kilarney*. The frail container then continued to swing wildly to and fro until the rope was cut.

With a young lad for company Brunel made the first official crossing in the basket at the end of September 1836. His new wife had declined to join him and must have thought she had made a wise decision when the haulage rope got jammed in the pulley and Brunel had to climb up from the swing-

ing basket to free it.

In 1851 the pressure of unpaid bills led to the sale of the bridge chains in 1853 and the bright hopes for the bridge again turning to despair. The iron bar still dangled from the gaunt and useless towers and for a time a small amount of income was derived from allowing people to cross at 5/- a time. Even in those days some young couples had a taste for an unusual wedding day and a pair of Failand newly-weds decided that a basket crossing would make their special day really memorable. This it did to a greater degree than they had expected for the haulage rope broke and they spent about an hour suspended high over the Avon Gorge and anxiously waiting for a new rope to be fixed.

The basket was subsequently removed but the iron bar was still to feature in a few more unusual moments. At this time in the 19th century it was fairly common practice for those politicians and others that had incurred public odium or displeasure to be hanged in effigy. And what more dramatic place than suspended from the iron bar high above the waters of the River Avon? In one such case the dangling figure proved an irresistible target for local marksmen who vied with one another to sever the rope and release the dummy into the river below. This was eventually achieved but the bar was then removed to discourage its further imaginative use by Bristolians.

The Lukins Affair

Lo, Lukins comes, and with him comes a train
Of Parsons famous for a lack of brain;
With owl-like faces, and with raven coats,
Their solemn step their task denotes,
By exorcising, prayers and rebukings,
To drive seven sturdy devils out of Lukins.

The affair of George Lukins, which came to a head at Temple Church in Bristol on 13 June 1788, split opinions in the city into firm believers and scornful sceptics. Lukins himself came from Yatton and was variously described as a carrier and a tailor. Whichever it may have been the man clearly had another side to his character. On the credit side he was apparently something of a singer and ventriloquist and also took part in the Christmas mummeries. On the other hand he was wont to display 'fits of howling and leaping' and to accuse various old people of bewitching him to their great embarrassment and distress.

Events in the Lukins affair came to a head in May 1788. The Rev. Easterbrook, vicar of Temple Church had previously tried to help Lukins but the latest appeal was couched in terms which demanded stronger action from a man of the minister's sincere beliefs. His lady caller from Yatton told him that:-

'she had seen a poor man afflicted with a most extraordinary malady, who when in fits would sing and scream in various sounds, scarcely human, and which fits to her knowledge he had been troubled with for near eighteen years. He had tried several medical gentlemen, but in vain. That the people of Yatton conceived him to be bewitched; that he himself declared he was possessed of seven devils, and that nothing could relieve him but the united prayers of seven clergymen who would ask for deliverance for him in faith.'

Thus it was that a fortnight later, on 'unlucky' Friday the thirteenth of all days, the Rev. Easterbrook, six other Wesleyan ministers and eight laymen assembled in the church vestry to carry out a service of exorcism. They began with hymns but this straight away produced a dramatic reaction from Lukins. His body began to convulse into extraordinary shapes and he leapt about uttering horrid blasphemies, sometimes in a deep threatening voice, sometimes in a high female tone. Then, sometimes singing, sometimes cackling, he boasted that he was 'the great devil' and chanted his master's praises while the ministers knelt in prayer. This process continued for a long time without any lessening of the tension and drama.

After nearly two hours of these extraordinary events signs of a change came when one minister repeatedly challenged Lukins to speak the name of Jesus. Consistently he responded with the word 'devil' until some of his spirit voices – or maybe his ventriloquist utterances – began to debate leaving his presence. More howlings and distortions eventually led to Lukins falling to his knees and praising God in his natural voice. Finally, after saying the Lord's Prayer, Lukins thanked his deliverers for the miracle of his abjuration.

Many people were unconvinced by this unusual case of apparent possession and exorcism. A Yatton surgeon was the leading scorner and he showered 'unsparing ridicule on the transaction, the actors therein and the man who he considered made them his dupes'. Even so, there are strong suggestions that Lukins was a changed man leading a sober Christian life among the Wesleyan society in Bristol for the rest of his life.

Ferries

Over the years at least fifteen ferry services have carried Bristolians back and forth over the city's waterways

Until bridge building came of age ferries played an important role in most large settlements built on a river and Bristol was no exception. Not that the life of an early ferryman was a sinecure; anything but, for the cream of his takings would go the owner of the ferry rights, those who could avoid using the ferry did so, and when it really became much used someone came along and built a bridge instead. Matters improved in Bristol when the Corporation took control of the ferries but it remained a hard manual job calling for experience and skill, especially on crowded waterways or those exposed to the wind and tides.

The senior Bristol ferry was the one at Rownham which was known to be in existence in 1148 when the Abbot of St Augustine acquired it to facilitate access to his Leigh residence. Even when Bristol Bridge was built the Rownham ferry still saved a long detour for those with business in the area below what is now the Cumberland Basin.

There was also a ford at Rownham and in 1610 two cases are recorded of horse riders drowning there while attempting to ride across the river. Later the ferry used a boat on which horses could be carried and became a favourite route for spa visitors out for a picnic on the meadows on the Rownham side. When the Corporation of Bristol acquired the Rownham Ferry in 1866 it had to pay the goodly sum of £10,000. Seven years later, as part of changes to the floating harbour entrance

locks, the ferry site moved some 200 yards upstream where its access slip is still visible despite closure of the route in 1932. In its later years the ferry provided a useful link between the trains serving Clifton Bridge station and the Cumberland Basin and Hotwells steamer landing stages and the trams on the Hotwells side of the Avon.

Another long-serving Bristol ferry was the one across the Avon from the tidal creek at Pill to the Lamplighters Inn on the Shirehampton side of the river. The packet service to and from Portishead called at these places and the ferry also provided a link with the railway lines which ran along each bank of the river and on into Temple Meads station. The Lamplighters Hotel, which gave its name to the ferry, dates from the middle of the 18th century and for many years was a popular destination for those taking a pleasure trip down river from Bristol. Still there, the hostelry owed its original existence to the profits made by a Mr Swetman in the course of providing lighting by oil lamps in many Bristol streets.

Several other ferries served inner Bristol before the major changes brought about by the construction of the floating harbour. The Gibb Ferry carried its patrons across the Avon at the end of Prince Street to what is now Wapping Road. For many years it was owned by the Dean and Chapter of the cathedral which continued to benefit from some of the tolls even when the ferry was replaced by a wooden bridge. Just a short distance upstream the Guinea Street Ferry carried people across to The Grove. Slips were provided in 1717 for the Guinea Street Ferry and for the one between Ferry Street, Redcliff Back and Welsh Back.

The ferry routes in Bristol reflected the changes and growth of the city itself. Before the destruction of the castle there was almost certainly a link from the Water

(Above) The River Avon looking downstream from the Cumberland Basin and with a paddle steamer leaving the Hotwells landing stage. The ferry across to Rownham is in the foreground.

(Below) In contrast to the rowing boat ferries of earlier years modern vessels now provide a service between the landing stages along the full length of the Floating Harbour.

(Above) The Shirehampton – Pill ferry in its
final years with Pill Creek and the railway
viaduct in the background. One ferryman is
at the oars, the other at the tiller.

(Below) The modern ferry service still uses
the Mardyke landing stage but the dark steps
and approach passage provide atmospheric
reminders of a different age.

Gate across to the Counterslip area. After the castle's demise and as the population on the St Philip side of the river rose rapidly during the 17th century a quicker cross-river route than that via Bristol Bridge became increasing imperative. A small-time entrepreneur responded by finding a rowing boat and introducing a ferry service across from Temple Back but the Corporation soon found out and in 1651 displaced him by introducing an authorised ferry route from Water Lane across to Cheese Lane for which it charged a rental of forty shillings a year. Traffic steadily increased until the numbers crossing well exceeded 100,000 a year with the ferry rights then being bought out by the company which opened St Philip's Bridge in 1841.

The completion of work on the Floating Harbour and its companion New Cut brought another change in the ferry scene at the beginning of the 19th century. The harbour was crossed by ferries from Prince's Wharf to Canon's Marsh, by the Wapping Ferry a little further west and which joined the appropriately-named Gasferry Road, to the gasworks end of Canon's Marsh, and by the Mardyke Ferry. The latter linked the Albion Dockyard area with Hotwell Road. Most of these ferries not only served the needs of their own local area but also formed part of through routes from the growing suburbs south of Coronation Road,

Two further ferries provided a service for passengers wishing to cross the New Cut. The Vauxhall Ferry was sited just west of the present footbridge linking the far ends of Coronation Road and Cumberland Road. Nearer the city the Gaol Ferry operated between the end of Dean Lane and the New Gaol which had its main entrance on the Cumberland Road. Users of this ferry had access to Wapping Wharf and the rest of the harbour area, to the warehouses, sheds and railway yards at the east end of Canon's

Marsh and on into the heart of Bristol itself. Bridges have now replaced the crossings of the New Cut and ended the Vauxhall, Gaol and Totterdown Ferries.

In the 19th century there were two boat crossings of the original route of the River Frome along St Augustine's Reach. One linked Broad Quay and St Augustines Parade and the other Narrow Quay with The Butts, now Canons Road.

Many traces of the old ferries still exist with a number of slips and steps remaining in remarkably good condition. Here the ferrymen of the past would sit on a thwart with their oars trailing in the water to collect the coppers from their passengers and whisk them on towards their various destinations. Happily Bristol still has a strong reminder of its traditional ferries in the modern service provided by the motor vessels of the Bristol Ferry Company whose calling points include a number of those used by ferry passengers over past centuries. A cross-river boat service from Beasey's Tea Rooms similarly commemorates the old ferry route between St Annes and Conham.

Against a background of modern housing the ferry vessel Brigantia of Bristol *approaches the old stone outer quay wall of the Mardyke ferry landing stage.*

Samuel Plimsoll

On an early summer day in 1898 a crew of sailors could be seen unhitching the horses from a hearse. They then proceeded to haul the hearse several miles to a churchyard. What led to such a demonstration of respect and affection? When one becomes aware that the person being buried was Samuel Plimsoll it becomes obvious why sailors, above all others, should wish to express their gratitude. They were honouring a man whose tireless campaigning led to safe loading lines being marked upon ships that dramatically improved the safety of seamen. Known as the Plimsoll Line it has now become a generic term for health and safety regulations. What was Samuel Plimsoll's background? What fostered in him a desire to relieve the suffering of an exploited workforce?

Samuel was born in 1824 in the Redcliffe district of Bristol. The Plimsoll family lived in Colston Parade overlooking the parish church of St Mary Redcliffe. His family was well established in Bristol, his maternal grandfather working as a shipwright and his paternal grandfather as a chandler. Samuel's father Thomas was employed as an excise man working out of an office in Queen Square. Thomas Plimsoll was married to Priscilla Willing and Samuel was the eighth of their thirteen children.

The family attended the local Congregational chapel and Samuel was baptised there, a few days before his first birthday. Samuel then remained a firm Congregationalist all his life and this was significant in the way he lived his life and the path he chose. The Congregational Church was dissenting in character, its members believing in personal responsibility and respecting authority only when exercised for the common good.

Samuel was three years old when Thomas and Priscilla Plimsoll moved the family to Penrith. He attended an infants school in the area. The family moved again, to Sheffield, when Samuel was in his fourteenth year. He left school at fifteen years of age and took up employment as a clerk in a solicitor's office. He next worked for Thomas Rawson, a brewer.

Tragedy struck when Samuel was sixteen years old. His father died, leaving this very young man with the responsibility for the support of his mother and five siblings. At seventeen Samuel rounded off his education by attending, part-time, The People's College, founded by the social reformer Robert Bayley. This stood him in good stead when he was invited to write speeches for one of the brewery partners, who happened to be the Mayor of Sheffield.

An attempt by Samuel to set himself up as a coal merchant ended in failure (due to the sharp practice of others) and he was declared bankrupt in 1855. It was during this bleak time that he was forced into charity accommodation, not the workhouse exactly, but degrading enough. Samuel was taken with the fact that the unemployed residents had a generosity of spirit, sharing their food and comforting one another. Although Samuel could not be described as disadvantaged or deprived in the accepted sense (he was, for example, well educated), he was to know poverty during this time. Whilst in the charity accommodation he rubbed shoulders with the poor and shared their privations. This enabled Samuel to have an understanding, a feeling, for the suffering of others. He eventually cleared his debts and went on to be a wealthy man (working again as a coal merchant) which of course, made it possible for him to devote himself to his political campaigns.

Although best remembered for the

Plimsoll Line, or more accurately the loadlines marked on the side of a ship that prevented overloading, Samuel was involved in other campaigns prior to his attempt to secure justice for seamen. He was a firm believer in public access to open spaces. As he was growing up the full impact of enclosures (the biggest single theft from the people in our history) was being felt by the rural and urban working class. The rural population in particular were grossly inconvenienced by the closure of former footpaths and Samuel supported their protest. He also campaigned to reopen footpaths already closed. Public access to open spaces became vital as towns and cities became more overcrowded and unhealthy. Although Samuel was not the only person to see the value of green spaces in urban areas and campaign for their protection, he was able to make a valuable contribution to the cause.

Mining was a particularly hazardous job in the nineteenth century. The workers toiling in this industry did so without adequate safety measures being in place. Samuel conducted various experiments to improve safety in the mines, particularly in detecting gas. He also raised money for injured miners and for wives and children of miners killed in pit disasters. In the Lund Hill pit disaster of 1857, a fire killed 189 people. Samuel organised the relief fund and over £10,000 was raised to relieve the suffering of the miners' dependants.

Legislation was necessary to improve the working conditions of miners, but this proceeded slowly, being blocked by vested interests and MP's compliant with these interests. They, of course, did not have to experience the risks undertaken by the miners, neither did they have to experience the risks undertaken by seamen. It was this understanding that led Samuel to campaign to improve the working conditions of seamen.

Samuel became active to improve the safety and working conditions for seamen on becoming MP for Derby in 1868. By that time he had married Eliza Railton. They had a daughter in 1865 who sadly died shortly after her birth. In 1866 they adopted their great niece, Nellie Plimsoll.

Samuel was certainly not the first or only person to campaign to prevent overladen vessels from sailing. He was, however, the most persistent (and perhaps the loudest) advocate. Reform during the nineteenth century was often resisted even if the appropriate legislation meant the saving of life. It was well known that many ships that foundered were overloaded. The loss of life was staggering, before and during the campaign for the adoption of loadlines. The shipowners (although there were a few honourable exceptions) and a compliant parliament opposed health and safety measures on the grounds that such regulations would give their overseas competitors an advantage over them. This was the same argument used by the opponents of the abolition of the slave trade and slavery. Even today the public needs to be vigilant in monitoring what a government does or does not do in its name.

Perhaps the greatest scandal was when heavily insured ships were sent to sea overloaded. Known as coffin-ships by the seamen they were naturally reluctant to sail in such vessels. Unfortunately for the sailors the Merchant Shipping Act of 1870 made refusal to sail on a ship punishable by a term of up to three months imprisonment. Although this only came into force once a sailor had 'signed on', many were 'signed on' without seeing the ship they were to sail in. The sailors, of course, knew best and could soon detect an unseaworthy ship. A refusal even in such circumstances made them guilty of an offence. Many chose prison. The police were also used to enforce the 'law', preventing sailors from leaving an unseaworthy ship. The press gang had returned to Britain.

Samuel Plimsoll's greatest strength in his fight to secure natural justice for seamen was his ability to harness public opinion to his cause. In the end it was the people that forced Parliament to do the right thing. This was quite an achievement when one considers that most of the population had no representation, being denied the vote. Public opinion and the mass of information collected by Samuel Plimsoll finally led to the passing of the 1876 Merchant Shipping Act. Every shipowner was ordered to mark, on the side of the ship, a circular disc with a horizontal line through its centre, down to which the ship might be loaded. This became known as the Plimsoll Line. The Merchant Shipping Act of 1890 legally enforced this convention.

Loadlines formed a 'ladder' on the sides of a ship which denoted levels of loading in varying conditions. The different levels were marked with initials representing Winter North Atlantic, Winter, Summer, Tropical, Freshwater and Tropical Fresh Water. All foreign ships leaving British ports were required to carry the same load-lines as British ships. This eventually led to the establishment of international regulations that are still in force today. These are regularly reviewed by the International

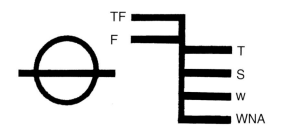

Maritime Organisation.

In 1882 Samuel's wife Eliza died. He married again in 1885, to Harriet Wade, when he was 61 years old. There were three children from this marriage, Samuel, Eliza and Ruth. Samuel Plimsoll continued to campaign for just causes to the end of his life. He supported moves to ensure adequate and better food for sailors, he was active in trying to improve the treatment of livestock on cattle ships, he was a firm advocate of Irish Independence and was a strong supporter of Trade Unions.

Samuel Plimsoll died in 1898. He had spent his life relieving distress wherever he found it. The causes he espoused were many and varied but he will chiefly be remembered for the mark that still saves lives today - the Plimsoll Line.

'Yo-
Ho-Ho
and a
boat
load
of
fun"

Bristol and the piracy tradition..........

THE LONG JOHN SILVER TRUST

was formed to promote Bristol's literary heritage and celebrate its links with Stevenson's classic novel *Treasure Island.* The trust's latest project is the 'Bristol Treasure Island Trail', a set of seven plaques around Bristol's harbourside telling the story of *Treasure Island* in a unique and innovative way.

To find out more about the trust visit www. longjohnsilvertrust.co.uk. To find out more about our new book on Bristol's pirates and privateers contact Fiducia Press.

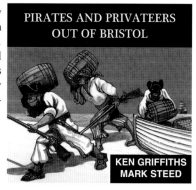

Public Transport in 1853

Thanks to *Wright's Bristol Steam Packet and Railway Timetables,* which could be purchased for just one penny in 1853, the people of Bristol could obtain all the information they might need to make their longer distance journeys. By this time the new railways had brought a wealth of new travel opportunities, the more astute coach operators had adjusted to their arrival by operating useful feeder routes and more reliable steam services had replaced sail on the services to and from the Bristol Channel ports.

By the year 1853 the Great Western and Bristol & Exeter Railways had linked London, Bristol and Exeter with connections at the latter for Plymouth, Truro and Penzance. Northwards there were trains to Gloucester and Birmingham which could be used to reach the North East and North West. From Gloucester the South Wales Railway ran south and then west through Chepstow, Cardiff and Swansea to Carmarthen. The best trains from Bristol to London took about three hours but the 10.50am service, which carried third class passengers, took eight. The former cost 26/1d first class and 18/3d second, the latter less than half that. The well-to-do could take their carriage and a pair of horses with them for a further 78/4d.

Stage coaches could no longer compete along the new railway routes but coach operators had fared well enough by serving the advancing railheads during the railway construction period and then filling in the gaps in the trains' coverage. From Bath, for example, there were two daily services to Wells with others to Weymouth, Poole and Salisbury. By changing from the train at Taunton one could journey on to either West Somerset or East Devon and other such routes linked Gloucester with Hereford and Brecon and Chippenham with Salisbury and Southampton. A network of multi-seat coaches, now with seats along the sides instead of across the vehicle, covered all the satellite communities around Bristol.

J.Bletchley of Thomas Street and D.Bennett & Co of the Counterslip were substantial carriers and would carry parcels and larger goods consignments to any main town within a radius of a hundred miles or so. Hewitt & Co's 'Universal Carrying Establishments' located at 6 Thomas Street, Bristol and the Old Bailey in London would accept a parcel of up to 7lbs for 3d or one of 2cwt for 3/9d. Special items such as musical instruments, toys, hats and furniture had to pay a premium. Many of the new carriers used the railways for the trunk journey and had an agent to undertake delivery at destination.

Better off people could hire a chaise or use their own but also had the alternative of using one of the many cabs which plied throughout the main areas of Bristol. From the newly-grown housing cluster extending up towards White Ladies Pike, for example, a cab would perform the trip to Bristol railway station for 1/8d. The fare from Horfield Barracks was a shilling more while two shillings covered a ride from the station to Clifton or to the 'Asylum for Deaf Mutes' in Redland.

The Wright timetables also published details of the cab fares for those wishing to use one of the numerous steamer services operating from Bathurst Basin and the adjoining Cumberland Basin, Rownham Ferry and Hotwells pontoons. The Old Company operated the *Dart* steamer to Newport and the *Swift* to Cardiff, both starting from Bathurst Basin and calling at Hotwells about 15 minutes later to collect the passengers from the waiting room opposite the landing stage there . Like all steamer operators the Old Company charged twice as much for seating in the aft cabin compared with the fore cabin while, somewhat surprisingly, Newport fares were three times those to Cardiff.

The Old Company also operated the steamers *Juno* and *Pheonix* to Tenby, the *Victory* to Waterford, the *Junerva* and *Sabrina* to Cork and the *Rose* to Dublin. The Swansea packet was the *Lord Beresford* and other vessels and companies served Newport and Cardiff along with Neath, Tenby, Carmarthen and Milford. Five services linked Bristol with Ilfracombe, Padstow and Hayle while local journeys between the Cumberland Basin and Portishead were catered for by the *Fairy Queen* for 1/6d return. This vessel called at Pill in one direction and the wharf near the Lamplighters Inn on the other with passengers then able to use the ferry that linked the two. Instead of using the Aust ferry or making the circuitous train journey via Gloucester there was the alternative of using the *Wye* steamer to cross the Severn estuary to Chepstow and then travel forward by coach or train.

Wright's timetables also contained extra pages devoted to other useful information and to advertising of one sort or another. Goods, services and accommodation all featured in its pages and a small section listed the vessels due to sail for Australia. These included the 111ton oak-built schooner *Active*, the 156ton oak-built 'Clipper Brigatine' *Prosperine* and the 214ton 'First Class Brig' *Jenny*. In the Postal Directory section things like post clearance times – a fairly general pattern of three clearances a day - and postal rates were recorded. Apparently the newspapers

As the railway network expanded in the mid-1800s the demand for connecting and other local services led to the appearance of increasing numbers of horse buses and other similar vehicles.

could be sent free to British possessions if conveyed by packet boat but cost a penny if carried on a private ship.

Among the feature material in this particular issue Hemming's Factory at Clift House, Bedminster commanded two illustrated pages. During his travels overseas the proprietor had seen a need for prefabricated buildings which could be shipped abroad in sections and erected on sites where materials, tools and constructions skills were in short supply. Soon the Hemmings firm was offering prefabricated houses, stores, warehouses, shooting boxes, schoolrooms and even hotels and churches, all erected on the Bedminster site for viewing and then offered free on board any ship sailing from Bristol.

Ostrich
on the Downs

In bygone centuries wild beasts certainly roamed over Bristol's Clifton and Durdham Downs but the 'ostrich' in this case refers to an inn once hugely popular with visitors to Durdham Down. In its 18th century heyday this hostelry catered for a clientele who represented a period of great change in the character of the natural downland areas on the high ground west of Bristol. It was a period when the two Downs, each totalling over 200 acres steadily left behind their pastoral years and an unsavoury period when they were home to vagrants and villains. Instead, in 1861, they became a permanent asset for public enjoyment thanks to a dedication of Clifton Down by the Society of Merchant Venturers and Bristol Corporation's purchase of Durdham Down.

Once the Romans no longer crossed the Downs to reach the little port of Abonae the area led a peaceful medieval existence as common pasture for the surrounding manorial communities. Apart from the spectacle of an occasional hanging its sheep grazed contentedly there until rudely disturbed by the soldiers of the Civil War. Then, in the second half of the 17th century, the area began to acquire an unsavoury reputation as a place to be avoided by honest folk. Disaffected and disadvantaged groups lived rough there and thieves and vagabonds preyed on anyone who crossed alone or in darkness.

Quite early on some stone had been quarried at scattered locations on the Downs and licences to allow individual miners to 'digge for leade' were granted as early as 1611. A century later there was an ambitious scheme to mine iron and lead ore, manganese and calamine and to build both storage sheds and a smelter. Nothing came

Pembroke Road used to be Gallows Acre Lane and executions took place here where it joins the Downs

of this but money had later to be spent on filling in the various mining and quarrying cavities created over the years.

In the first half of the 18th century the Downs began to change in character. The sinister side remained with the first turn-piked roads out of the city towards Westbury and Stoke Bishop having their gates broken down by rioters and troops having to be brought in to protect them. A soldier was shot for desertion on the Downs in 1728, five murderers were executed on the gallows in the early 1740s and several robbers suffered the same fate. At the same time the wealthier city merchants, seeking a more pleasant climate than that offered down in the city, began a period of building fine houses in Clifton and the Downs began to be used for sports and entertainment more frequently and in a more organised way.

The tradition of horse racing on Durdham Downs began early in the 18th century. It grew increasingly popular and created a tradition that lasted for over a hundred years. By the 1830s the original course had been greatly improved and provided with accommodation for spectators to enjoy the traditional Easter and May events, with thousands coming to watch the races and bet on the outcome. There were also fringe attractions including gambling tents and vendors of every sort.

In addition to the new houses on the fringes of Clifton the popularity of the Hotwell spa added to the change in character of the Downs. There were customers aplenty for the Ostrich Inn which soon became the fashionable place to visit. After taking the waters early in the morning the richer and more socially inclined of the spa visitors could take to their horse or carriage to visit the Ostrich and recover there by consuming one of its advertised early breakfasts. One of the more enterprising owners even installed a number of lanterns outside the Ostrich for the benefit of later visitors who came for a day or evening excursion and stayed until late to enjoy its food, warmth and comfort.

Backsword contests were also staged on Durdham Down. This was an especially bloody sport won by the contestant 'breaking the most heads' with his cudgel. The Ostrich Inn was ever ready to slake the thirst of the watchers and bind up the injured.

It also had its own cockpit for cockfighting devotees. The custom was for teams from different localities to compete under quite specific rules and with quite substantial prize money at stake, anything from 3 to 5 guineas a fight and up to 60 guineas for the owner of the bird which won the final. In 1778 for example the Ostrich cockpit was host to teams from Devon and Somerset in which each side presented 51 cocks and stood to win up to 350 guineas.

At various times both men and women competed in foot races, boxers pounded one another into submission, fancy dress and other processions or parades took place and various bands added their music to the celebrations. All good for business at the Ostrich.

As building on the original downland resumed after the Napoleonic Wars and its surface was continually scarred by quarrying and other excavations the movement to protect the area grew in strength. Initially the Society of Merchant Venturers appointed a Conservator for Clifton Downs while the City Council took the imaginative step of purchasing some tenements within the Manor of Henbury in order to become a commoner with both a voice in Durdham Downs matters and the right to graze sheep there! The eventual outcome was the Clifton & Downs Act which received the Royal Assent in 1861 and protected these precious open spaces for ever.

𝖘𝖆𝖓𝖈𝖙𝖚𝖆𝖗𝖞

For around a thousand years anyone fleeing from the law could take refuge in a church and claim the protection of its sanctuary. This concept of sanctuary was rooted in the intrinsic status of the altar, a spot made holy by the presence of God and therefore not to be violated. All churches offered the right of sanctuary to anyone accused of a felony once they had reached a defined point. This could be the altar itself, the ffrith or peace stool nearby, a sanctuary knocker on the church door or even, in some cases, the stones or wall that marked the boundary of consecrated ground. Some senior churches could offer shelter to those accused of more serious crimes by virtue of a special charter from the monarch.

In 13th century Bristol one William de Lay sought to invoke protection in this way by fleeing from the wrath of Peter de la Mare, at that time constable of Bristol Castle. He managed to reach the churchyard of St Philip & St Jacob and must have breathed a sigh of relief once inside its walls. By custom achieving sanctuary meant safety and protection since not only was the church involved under a strict duty to provide food and shelter for the fugitive but anyone planning to breach the right of sanctuary risked excommunication, execution or both. Similarly there might be penalties for the community if the accused person was allowed to escape.

If matters had followed their proper course William de Lay, whilst safe, would have become enmeshed in a rigorous procedure that involved confessing his transgression and agreeing either to stand trial or 'abjure the realm' within forty days. In the latter case his possessions were forfeit to the church and his property to the crown. Then, simply robed, barefoot, bareheaded and carrying a cross to denote the protection of the church, he was required to take a specified route to the coast and take passage on the first available vessel there. The unhappy man was not permitted to deviate from his route nor to stay more than two nights in any one place on the journey.

So much for the system. In practice many fugitives just slipped away at the first opportunity and automatically became outlawed. Others were rescued by friends or accomplices while not a few were snatched from sanctuary by those they had wronged. William de Lay was one of the latter. The constable's men dragged him from the church by force and threw him into a prison cell inside the castle. Worse was to come for he was later beheaded.

When news of this gross breach of sanctuary reached the ears of the Bishop of Worcester he quickly took action against the perpetrators. The bishop held the devastating power of excommunication which made it nigh impossible to resist any punishment he might impose. Peter de la Mare, despite his own high office, was punished by being ordered to erect a stone cross beside the castle moat and there feed a hundred poor people on an appointed day each year. He also had to pay for a priest to celebrate mass every remaining day of his life. Nor did the men involved in snatching the sanctuary claimant escape the bishop's wrath. On four market days they were made to walk from Lewin's Mead to the scene of their unlawful behaviour, clad only in shirt and breeches and flogged every inch of the way.

The practice of sanctuary declined rapidly after the Reformation being greatly restricted in an Act of 1540 and virtually abolished in another of 1623.

Gaol

'White without and foul within'

In the past justice was not the measured process it is today and those who fell foul of the law and were sent to prison had to endure great privations in addition to the loss of freedom. Bristol's gaols were no exception as this 1787 quote indicates

The first Bridewells were houses of correction for short term offenders such as vagrants and those committing petty offences. Vagrants were the bane of the Middle Ages and the Bristol establishment in Bridewell Lane was extended in the 1620s by the addition of a mill and workhouse to put them to productive work. Later it was the focal point for the persecution of Quakers and other dissenters who were confined in terrible numbers and circumstances.

Bristol had several local prisons to serve the local courts but the main and most notorious place of incarceration was Newgate which housed both felons and debtors. The conditions there were awful with corruption, fever, poor food and little sanitation the norm. There were dark, damp, subterranean cells for the condemned and cages for the rowdy.

In 1820 Newgate was replaced by the New Gaol which boasted a treadmill for raising water among its amenities but both the latter and the Bridewell were seriously damaged in the Bristol Riots in 1831. The rioters kept battering the gates until a small boy was able to slip inside and let the mob in to fire the premises and release some 170 of its inmates

Although repaired the New Gaol steadily deteriorated and was eventually closed in 1833 when its role was taken over by the new state prison at Horfield and the site sold to the Great Western Railway in 1895 at a time when the company was planning the extension of its harbour lines. But the frontage has survived and remains as a stark reminder of the past and some of the dreadful scenes played out here.

Shortly after the opening of the gaol on the New Cut John Horwood was hanged in the gate building for the murder of Eliza Balsum near Hanham Mill. Despite a plan for a boat rescue of the body it went to the Royal Infirmary for dissection with the skin then being used to cover a book detailing the surgeon's findings and poor John's trial. Equally poignant was the last hanging at this place, that of 17-year old Sarah Harriet Thomas in 1849. As was the unseemly custom of the times both executions had been carried out in the full view of crowds lining the New Cut.

The derelict gateway of this old prison remains a sad reminder of the hangings which were once a public spectacle for crowds lining the New Cut.

William West

*'his labour and ingenuity
was thrown away'*

William West, the subject of this comment in 1835 and the creator of the camera obscura on the Downs, was a man of many parts. As well as being an artist of the Bristol School he was an amateur scientist with a considerable knowledge of optics and sufficient of an engineer to put forward quite sound ideas for achieving completion of the Clifton Suspension Bridge when the work on Brunel's scheme ran out of money.

West was born in 1801 and started off his adult life in the dyeing business. He was

The Observatory occupies a vantage point high on the Downs, chosen when it began life as a windmill.

sufficiently well off to spend an increasing amount of time painting and at the age of twenty seven he rented the site and ruins of an old windmill on top of Clifton Down. The windmill had originally been built by one James Waters on land rented from the

Society of Merchant Venturers in 1766 but just two years later had caught fire in a gale when strong winds had whirled the sales around so fast that the primitive wooden friction brake could not restrain them and the timbers had caught fire. The connection with fire was maintained during the Napoleonic Wars when the site was chosen for a beacon to give warning of any French invasion.

Seized by the exciting possibilities of his acquisition West immediately set about making the old windmill ruin fit for his family to live in. His plans included refurbishing the main original round building and adding above it an observatory which included a revolving dome to house his telescopes, the height of the building offering an unrestricted and dramatic view in all directions. This also made it ideal for the camera obscura he installed, its lens reflecting the surrounding landscape onto a shallow viewing dish. One of West's best-known watercolours depicts the main building and an elaborate extension he planned.

Opening onto the cliff face of the Avon Gorge at a point in St Vincent's Rocks quite near West's old windmill was a natural cave known as the Giant's Cave, believed once to have been the access to a hermitage. To add to the public attraction represented by the camera obscura West set about creating underground access to the cave, reaching it in 1835 and completing the works in readiness for visitors two years later. Out of the ruins of the fire ravaged windmill he had now created the home in which he was to live until his death in 1861, a place in which to pursue his interests and two attractions to offer Bristolians.

Not far from the building West was renovating an even more exciting project was coming to life. The money left by Alderman Vick for the building of a bridge across the Avon Gorge had, by 1829, grown